Forged

Relic

A Book of Poems

Andrew Howe

To my wife that was there even in my darkest moments.

Contents

Poems of War

These poems came from my time in the Navy. Hearing stories from friends or watching the news. War changes everyone that's involved and never for the better, most of these are dealing with going into battle or what's left after a war.

The Battlefield

How far will I be able to go
To lift this sword and shield
Who can see friend or foe
Will I be the same after the field

Someone told me to follow
All I end up is hollow
My armor can't withstand the cold
All I can do is what I am told

There is no winner in a fight
These scars will live with me
But can I rely on my sight
To save me in this war

I can be brave
I can be honorable
I can believe
I can lose my soul

I held my sword with the world
I blocked with my shield through hope
Every hit I took I took for freedom
Every person I bested I did to live

But how can I live with the guilt
The lost lives
The lost days
The lost families

This is a world forged by weapons
We need to take our loses
Bury our friends that lost their lives
To repair the world and heal

From Ruins to Life

Foundation was never sound
Right location was never found
Only buildings lay in rubble
Memories just lying in ruins

Rather then restoring it
Untouched by any hands
Infected by the lives around
No peace ever came here
So nature claimed it as its own

Those that lived here are left to nourish
Once time has passed life grows freely

Left with beautiful flora over its history
It seems like life takes shape over ruins
Fixing once was a great city
Every life lost helps life to grow

Snowfall

I walk around an empty town
Just on my own
The snowfall covers the streets
Only my heartbeats
All I see is a blanket of snow
To end the sorrow

I can see where my future lies
My destination
Footprints being my narratives
My desolation
The past steps lie and wait
My motivation

The street lights emits a cold glow
Reflecting off the snow
Too much makes it hard to breath
Brings so much death
The empty town burns so bright
Black clouds the moonlight

Another town lost to our own fires
The ashes hides our desires
Everything seems to have lost its colors
A town that has ruined its futures

Silent Town

I run my fingertips along the wall
Feeling all the holes and cracks
Looking at all the lost pictures
So much history still stands tall

All the windows shattered
All the memories scattered
All the rooms plundered
Homes became a biohazard

The house seems frozen in time
Just the sounds of creaks
Years since it's been lived in
Hasn't been a home in a lifetime

War has left its disease
Wasteland with living trees
Plant life hiding the bodies
Bombs didn't care for these families

Every old home lost to poison
There's no do over for what was done
A silent town
A quiet town

A whole town lost to war
We can't take back what was done
A empty town
A hollow town

Adaptable

Adapting became so easy
Changing to whatever life needs
Haven't you been able to see
Living in plain sight
Just isn't right

If the world floods
Would I not float
If it flows lava
Would I not fly
If the earth shakes
Would I not adjust

Altering one self to blend in
Camouflage to blend with the crowd
Haven't you been able to feel
Living in plain sight
Just isn't right

So many personalities to juggle
Which one seems believable
Haven't you been able to tell
Living in plain sight
Just isn't right

When you see me
Would I not mould
When speaking to me
Would I not act the part
When gathered around
Would I not adjust

It's not as easy as changing a shirt
Able to move in the background
Haven't you been able to watch
Living in plain sight
Just isn't right

Being in a new place
Do I not learn
Being approached
Do I not calculate
Being questioned
Do I not adjust

I must continue
I will mould
I will fold
I must get through
I will heal
I will deal

I must breakthrough
I will grow
I will flow

When it's time to be another person
I rebuild on what's left of the last memory
Haven't you been able to hear
Living in plain sight
Just isn't right

When do I stop fixing myself
When do I start being myself
How to tell when it's all enough
How to tell when I'll be enough

Grey World

It's a new world I live in
A world where heroes become villains
The old world was black and white
Just so many live in the gray area

When did the world crumble to pieces
Our hearts are always in a heightened state
The lives we lost will never be forgotten
It's our constant wars that leave us empty

Our gray world needs more color
It's being painted by our tears
With the red spilled from our friends
Then the green from all our greed

I live in a broken world
A discolored world
A lost world
Not in the world I knew

Where can we go from here
We shouldn't live in fear
Needs outweigh the caring
It's the new world we live in

The Guilt

The cries I still hear
The whispers I fear
The friends that are still there
Those never left my prayer

If I held out my hand
Would you pull me up
Or let me live in the sand
The life that developed

I never left what's behind me
I should never have left
I was not meant to leave
I wasn't supposed to grow old

It's been me alone
I never forgot my friends
Holding onto everyone
I will never make these amends

The fallen never left me
The faith never left me
The silence never left me
The guilt never left me

Poems of
Hope

Most of these came from a place feeling hopeless. People have always lived with problems and the stress that comes with everything. I just want the best for everyone that thinks they are alone in a scary world.

Lasting Forest

I was once a house for many critters
I could hear birds sing their love songs
I provided a place to relax after adventures
Now I can see my friends lying around me

I've had pictures taken from every season
People would come and make beautiful paintings
For any looking to hide I provided protection
Now all the colors we shared became so faded

I was once lush
Now I'm colorless
I was once beautiful
Now I'm scarred
I was once alive
Now I'm rotting

I've watched generations grow up all around me
I would watch baby animals take their first steps
I could hear the cries of little ones being hungry
Now there is no sounds, no smiles, no one around

I can remember the piercing cracks
And thundering crash as we come to rest
To make room for more people to live
But I know while I leave, more of us are being
sprouted

Perfect Storm

They say a captain goes down with his ship
To have everything slip through their fingertips
The crew carries the weight of the fellowship
What is there to do when all holds slip

All it takes is the perfect storm
The worst thunderstorm
The coldest lullaby
The hardest goodbye

Hope in the faces of friends
Hope dries up your amends
Hope helps with ascends
Hope defines what defends

There is no wave we can't handle
So few are more accountable
We hold tight so we won't crumble
They know things have gone critical

They trust me with their lives
I have lived in their eyes
It's me that will hear their cries
My job to prevent our capsize

Hope did not leave us that night
Hope gave us the will to fight
Hope helped us to rewrite
Hope took control of the firefight

A Friend

I need a friend for the end of the world
Not to sleep with
Not to fall in love with
But to yell with the world

I need someone to take on the world
Not to die with
Not to lose myself with
But to cry with the world

No need to out live the present
Tomorrow is a future that never comes
Today is my day to smile wide
Today is a day we just survive

I need a hand for the end of the world
Not for holding
Not for rebuilding
But for wiping the tears from the world

Feel the sun's warmth
Hear the flowing river
Smell the growing flowers
To close your eyes and breathe in the world

I need a friend for the end of the world
Not to change with
Not to survive the gloom with
But to smile, laugh, and enjoy the world

Deserving

Don't feel like its worth it
There's so much you do
That you don't see
Behind the scenes

I do feel like you're worth more
You deserve much more
You just don't see
More than your means

The world needs a stranger
Like you
It's the insight you bring
No clue
What the world can bring you
It's true

It's when the world goes dark
The world will need your light
Hope you will see your spark
Just show others how bright

There was just so much taken away
So much everyday

What I want to tell you is that
Everything that you hope for
Will come true my friend

Running

I wanted to let go
I wanted to forget
I wanted piece of mind
I wanted to be free

I left it all behind me
I held onto my thoughts
I was filled with an urge
I packed up and walked out

I walked to an open field
I held out my hand
I felt the tips of grass
I can see the flowers flow

I can see no future here
I don't seem to mind though
I see wind blowing through the trees
I slowly take another step

I hold my breath for another step
I feel the ground crunch below
I pick up the pace to feel the wind
I can feel no weight of my past

I can see the wind over the grass
I am just running as fast as I can
I enjoy the wind coming at my face
I am running to leave it all behind

I can feel tears flowing down
I can feel myself being lost
I can feel my heart racing
I can feel that I am free

Home

It started with a dream
To build a house for his family
I helped him build our house
It brought so much happiness

I lived in the house we built
It felt like home for many years
Longer I lived there alone
Less of a home it felt

This was a home for my father
His last breath was in his room
Now the house has lost its color
Seems we built a tomb

Then one day she happened
Helped to fix a forgotten home
I no longer felt abandoned
The house needed love

I carried her through the doors
Of our home
Years filled the empty rooms
Of our home
We created our heirloom
From our home

I know this home will be with our family
For generations to come
Laying here in peace reliving our memories
From our family album
All was needed was our love to fix this house
Make it our home

I Tried

I walk up to a fear of mine
I hold out my hand, feel the smooth lines
My heart racing as I see my seat
I look at the road ahead, long journey

I will take deep breaths
I will hold tight
I will not fail
I will try

I get comfortable where I'm sitting
So many lights, buttons and switches
I ran through so many simulations
I know I can do this, I will do this

I will fly this plane
I will stay calm
I will not fail
I will try

I tried to push my boundaries
I tried to not lose control
I tried to find myself

I tried to be me
I tried to fly
I tried to
I tried

No other feeling like being free in the sky
All seems so peaceful, with the horizon
Everyone is counting on me to land safely
This pilot will see that everyone makes it through

Our Memories

The memories that we hold close
We hold dear
They never seem to be the same
Be the hope
Should we keep the ones that turn
Ones that change
Is it healthy to let go of the old ones
The old memories

Why do we hold on to a memory
Ones that can only bring sadness
Why show us our own regrets
Leave the ones we want to forget

Why do we have ones that trigger pain
That trigger loss
Even the thoughts that brings us tears
Bring us happiness
How to erase the hold of bad images
Of bad thoughts
Would it be a good idea to press reset
To press restart

Our memories made us who we are
Our trials, our faults, the things we overcame
They created each individual person
They created me, you, and us

Little Firefly

No amount of makeup
Can cover up your scars
Every time you smile
I can see your tears
You've given the world enough
Live the rest of your years

It might seem like a hollow love
What else do you need to prove
You don't require a shell anymore
Spread your wings and just soar

No need to yell into your pillow
No need to be afraid of your shadow
No need to shudder from below
No need to shiver from an echo

It's never easy to say goodbye
Leaving a past that wounds you
Time to be yourself again little firefly
Grow bright and make your own light

Generations

I was rocked asleep every night
Being held and just letting go
My dad always holding me tight
Feeling safe when held in his arms

The rocking chair that held memories
All the scratches gave it personalities
My first memory was being gently rocked
Dad just has the biggest smile when I wake

Chair stood still the day he passed away
Mom and I lost days staring at an empty chair
I wanted to feel safe so I climbed into it yesterday
Never has a chair felt like home with a sway

Those were some of the hardest years
What felt so safe brought even more fears
How could he just leave us alone
Left us with a chair that stayed at home

Years past and I forgot about his rocking chair
It was left with mom and I know she cared
So hard to see a empty seat everyday
I never wanted to see his favorite chair bare

I told my mom I was having a baby, a son
Few weeks later I heard a knock, at home
I opened the door and I felt a tear, run down
I stood frozen as he was here, right now

Mom told me you will need this for your son
I was my father's daughter and I remember
I felt safe in his arms being rocked away
I never thought I would see it to my dismay
A note was carved for me under the seat

My grandfather's note
To my son who I always rocked asleep
I finished this the day you arrived

My father's note
To my daughter that I never wanted to let go
Keep this chair memory alive as I did

The rocking chair that held memories
All these scratches gave it personalities
My sons first memory was being gently rocked
Shows the biggest smile when he wakes

Now the chair will continue to rock

Hiding Away

I can see you hiding in the corner
Hiding away from the world
You can come out now, it's over
The darkness is no longer

I can see you crying in your room
Holding onto the last word
Let the tears flow, they speak volume
They will help a flower bloom

I can see you losing yourself again
Leaving behind your smile
The life you once lived is arcane
Please come back to this domain

Distraction
Only works for so long
Satisfaction
You will become whole
Celebration
For what comes next

I can see you happy once more
Moving onto brighter things
To be the one that works to restore
You will get that big encore

Poems of Loss

These are the hardest poems for me to write. These ones always make me sad when I think about them. They are from watching the news about different shootings. They are from personal experiences. I can't imagine the feelings people go through dealing with the loss of a loved one. Everyone deals with loss differently.

The Reruns

I see the faces of futures taken away
The smiles that were taken away
The missing of loved ones
All we see is more reruns

Empty caskets fill the grounds
All remains is head stone mounds
To many heavy abductions
We still hear about the reruns

Being held up by so many pictures
None show the soulless abductors
Broadcast the disruptions
Stop making these reruns

So many tears flowing down
Feel the loss all over town
The heartache is all around
Yet the reruns won't breakdown

The White Bed

The white bed in a empty room
The last room you will lay
The glow haunts the cold gloom
The silence continues every day

Sickness left you pale
Gasping makes you frail
Reaching the end of your tale
Holding on to the last exhale

The life you lived
The stories you told
The troubles you survived
The hearts that you consoled

Next stop is your gate
This has been your fate
Leave your emotional weight
There is no need for the wait

The white bed in a empty room
The sounds of the loving cries
The passing lifting up the gloom
The last spoken words are goodbyes

Never Forget

I remember the day you moved across the street
The first time you smiled at me
The first time we went to the park
The first time we held hands

I remember the day we first kissed
The first time we slept together
The first time we told our parents
The first time I said I loved you

I remember the day we got married
The first day we heard the news of war
The first day we became brothers in arms
The first day we survived our fight

I remember the day you left this world
The first night you weren't there to help
The first morning I woke up screaming
The first week after the war was won

I wish I could see you again
I wish I could go back as kids
I wish I could forget all this pain
I wish I could live my life

I remember my best friend
I remember my brother
I remember my lover
I will never forget

A Rose Decor

I was handed rose seeds
On the day she loved me
Growing together with a rose bush
It seemed to always flourish

Keeping it alive with its thorns
Never hurt that much
But we always kept it watered
Watched it blossom in the sun

As time went on thorns hurt more
More then just our décor
Forgetting to water the soil
The dying rose bush was loyal

It held on to the last flower
While we fought for asylum
Sheds it petals like tears
Falling from the weight of the world

Every argument felt like our last
The rose bush always held fast
When I closed the door for the last time
Last petal hit the floor felt a lifetime

Never has a plant died so alone
So cold
Every petal just swept away
So dry

The décor just wilts in the corner
Hard to see what was there
How to fix something timeless
Memories of love and happiness

Emptiness
Emotionless
My last loveless night
Loneliness
Sleeplessness
My last loveless fight

Heartbreak
Heartache
My last loveless night
Mistake
Outbreak
My last loveless fight

Intoxicated Ride

I'm not made of steel
I can't stop a moving car
My wounds take time to heal
Every cut leaves a scar

I want to be the one that helped
I wish to protect
I wish to stop what happened
I have carried this loss too long
I wish to forget
I wish to live a life where I belong

I'm not made from hope
I can't reappear anywhere
My life is under a small scope
Every night is a nightmare

I can bring hope
I can bring wishes
I can bring dreams
I can bring me

Sorry a driver ended a life
It's not right to lose everything
In a instant nothing will be the same
But you have your life still holding on

Last words

I've watched the images of my past
I know what it was like to feel complete
I've felt my life left me too fast
My heart is coming to its final beat

I see the one that will hold my hand
I feel relief that I'm out of falling sand
The reaper will help me cross the planes
Please take away all my crippling pains

This is where your timeline comes to a close
Is there any thought you want disclose
What did my life leave for our tomorrow
Did I leave the world behind full of sorrow

You have left behind your heavy heart
Carrying the weight of the world falls apart
Afterwards the memories of you will live
Many will tell stories of your perspective

Do you know where I will go when I leave
Was it enough for me that I did believe
You believing is what kept you breathing
It's time you are free for your final resting

You lived a full life
You lived a blessed life
You lived a great life
You lived a life

Haunted Memories

I found myself on empty streets
Even though they were once so busy
Now it's just silence that haunts them
Left with crumbled homes and lives

Through the forests that once had laughter
Now the trees are stained from fallen friends
Any evidence will be grown over and forgotten
Left with a haunted memory of once was

Even when you survive
You lose yourself
Even when you're sleeping
You dream nightmares
Even when you're home
You are left alone
Even when seeking help
You will never forget

Sitting down in what used to be your favorite chair
Being surrounded by family and friends
Now not even able to communicate with them
Left with a fake smile that I have to practice

Good bye

How is it
That you took so much from me
How is it
You can't take time to see me
How is it
The words you spoke broke me

It's not like you left
Was I too much for you
I'm holding on to the cliff
Were you too much for me
Might be good to drift

Could it be
You were to scared of me
Could it be
That pain was easier then me
Could it be
Your heart beat was held by me

Set me free
Of your hold you left on me
Set me free
The mind you stole from me
Set me free
It is your touch that scares me

Not like you were there
Was it too hard to hold on
My footing can't be left bare
Did I hold on to hard
Should I stop and be fair

Where were you
To wipe the tears from me
Where were you
Just to say you're here for me
Where were you
Drive my anger away from me

I think I lost myself in you
I had to breathe without you
I wound up gone and lost
I felt a beat that skipped past

Want to say
You won't be a ghost by me
Want to say
Life wont be the same with me
Want to say
Good bye

Last Breath

When the time came to live
The call came in
The cries came in

All it took was one accident
To change a life
To scar a life

Living in a world that's shattered
A second to fade
A heart to fade

How to forget the moment
That changed the future
How to forgive the moment
That changed the future

Where do you look for shelter
A place to heal
A place to feel

Can one forget the impact
That changed the future
Can one forgive the impact
That changed the future

Where did the old soul vanish
Could one grow up
Could one grow hope

A blink of an eye is all it takes
For the world to change
Yet it continues to spin
It's about start over for someone

Every breath is a challenge
It's the hardest breath to take
The last breath to exhale
To be able to breathe in the fresh new air

Empty Soul

There were no screams when the glass broke
Even when the bullet broke through
No one spoke

All that remains is a hole in a glass pane
What was used to see the outside world
Full of pain

A life is never worth taking without any remorse
Without any feeling
Without any thought
Without any knowing

Now what is left is a gone soul laying on the floor
A lost wife
A lost sister
A lost mother

What's left is a broken world
Because a broken person
And now an empty hole
From a empty person

Us Versus The World

You were supposed to be invincible
You were the athletic one
You always lived so careful
It was supposed to be
Me and you versus the world

I never did win a race against you
I never stood in the way of your dreams
I always cared about you
It should always be
Me and you versus the world

I always felt your love towards me
I always hoped this world would help you
It shouldn't have ended this way
It has been in my eyes
Me and you versus the world

When the sickness took hold
This reality became too cold
The air quality turned to mold
Why didn't we have the
Stronger walls for our stronghold

I remember our lunches
I remember our walks
I will hold onto your memory
We lost my hero to a illness
Me and you versus the world became empty

Last Flicker

When I look into your eyes
I watch our memories disappear
And our life told by lies
With a life living in fear

When I hear your voice
I remember how the times were
I know with time not by choice
It all seems to fade into a blur

I know who you are
Who you were
I know how you were
How you cared

How long will it to take to forget
I see that time hasn't been great
So how can you leave our duet
Struggling to even be there

I don't want you to meet me again
Don't introduce yourself to me
Future memories will hold me to this plane
I want to see how to repair

Too many memories to hold on to
The brighter lights will dim
But I will never let them go
The world seems so grim
But never while you were here

I know who you are
Even though you forgot me
Who you were
Even though I'm missing there
I know how you were
Even though you forgot me
How you care
Even though I'm missing there

Just don't let the last light flicker off

The Fallout

Out of nowhere
It was a blink when it happened
The ripples were felt across the city
The epicenter where one was lost
So much was gone but at what cost

Ones closer to her
We're caught in fear
Her family lost so much
Everyone felt her touch
Friends were shaken
With the life that was taken
But was still felt by all
No one could stop the fall

Out of everybody
Who could've seen it coming
It was so heartbreaking
So much destruction
It was all put in motion

News got around
Fell silent across the world
It was so heartbreaking
So much destruction
There was no sign of caution

All that remains is the radiation
No matter how long
There is no vaccination

Out of everybody
No one could have stopped it
Pulled trigger changed our hearts
We knew to build the ramparts
Did it have to lay so much damage

No shelter
For this fallout
No cover
For this fallout
No hiding
From this fallout
No running
From this fallout

She never got the chance
To change the world
She never got the chance
To speak a word
She never got the chance
To say goodbye

Forged Relic

It started with a tree
Beautiful and free
Growing strong
Where it belongs

But with such beauty
Comes with misery
The island where the tree stood
Where people grew up good

The island couldn't withstand
A hurricane
Washed all that remained
With mighty rain
It seems nature left its mark
Brought only pain

This tree that once sheltered life
Now being pulled and dragged
Left to be rotten
Left forgotten

Then one day it wasn't taken
By the water
It had become awakened

By the weather
If only it wasn't mistaken
By one another

As the tree lays there washed up
A little girl walks with her new family
The loss of her old family scared her voice
Nothing left to say by her own choice

Family grew when they adopted
They knew it would be complicated
But they loved her
Like their own daughter

The girl saw what's left of this tree
Recognized it even with the debris
She ran her finger tip down the tree
Tears slowly rolls off her cheek beautifully

Fingers stop at the carvings that were left
It was her family
The feeling of anger, sadness and bereft
Screamed painfully

Initials of
Father, mother and brother
The love of
Father, mother and brother

She wanted to be so strong
Shedding a tear seemed wrong
Crying made the loss so real
Now she can grow and heal

Then felt a sudden warm hand
Followed with a warm embrace
None of this was planned
We were luckily in the right place

Parents never heard a word from her
Till this day and it was a scream
They held their embrace till closure
The parents knew what this means

Without talking speaks volume
They carried what's left of her old family
To hang up in their living room
So she can now live happily

A lost tree
Forged into a relic
Brought back a voice
And made a family closer

A reminder of what once was
To healing what is
Making way for the future

Fallen Down

I fell down
I turned to screaming
A sense of fear came over
Instantly felt great loss

My friend came to help
When she reached for me
Her touch couldn't be felt
I could only sense her

Why did she leave me alone
Where was her thinking going
What did the world do to you
How did I not see past your smile

The sadness you held
The guilt I feel
I wasn't there for you
But you were here for me

Not a day goes by
Without a tear
I miss my friend
But I will grow

Poems of Depression

These poems are personal for me. It's me trying to navigate the different emotions. Most of these took me a long time to figure out how to deal with some of these events. This is just me trying to figure out how to be human again.

Parasitic Voices

Each voice calls me by a different name
Ghost, antagonist, loner, outcast, idiot, lame
Too many to know which one is right
No matter what I do I hear the parasite

It's stealing my soul
It's leeching my life
It's taking my temple
It's driving my depression

My soul is cracked and missing pieces
Too many fragments left on the floor
Still filling in the holes from my voyages
My internal voices always at an uproar

This life is draining what's left of being human
So much pretending leaves me exhausted
What gave me hope became abandon
One day I know these voices will be faded

The temple that I escape to, heals me
It's not working as well as it's used too
How can I reach something overseas
Can't anyone hear what I'm going through

Thriving depression took my smile
The consuming darkness must be stopped
Having hope changes my lifestyle
Raising freedom need to be dropped

A Magic Trick

Did you know I can do magic
It doesn't have to be a tragic
The trick that deserves a premiere
I can make myself disappear

If one is gone
Would one be home
If lost I'm done
To be all alone

When the spell has been cast
All the heart beats will last
Some time the mind will send fear
I can make myself disappear

Seems so out of reach for others
So many that came before weren't losers
Is it to hard for everyone to hear
I can make myself disappear

Would all my problems just dissolve
What's worse is no one can evolve
A way to make my mind clear
I can make myself disappear

One can't feel touch
It's all too much
I'll be a stranger
Out of my danger

Did you know I can do magic
It doesn't have to be a tragic
The trick that deserves a premiere
I can make myself disappear

Instrumentality Wasteland

Is this glass box big enough
Why can't I see it
Why can't I break it
Put in the glass box from grief
Will it ever get bigger
Will it ever get smaller

Just so tired being locked away
I deserve the isolation
The time fades just like the day
I deserve the destruction
Stuck in this instrumentality wasteland

Why can't anyone hear when I yell
Living in a soundproof room
People seem to walk by and stare
No key is needed for this tomb

The glass box isn't getting warmer
Always so cold
Always to mold
World outside seemed to be getting louder
It's drowning
It's damaging

So tired of being locked away
I deserve this creation
Today seems so far from yesterday
I deserve this desolation
Stuck in this instrumentality wasteland

The rocking
The shaking
Why can't I breathe
The living
The lying
Just piling on

The walking
The yelling
No where to go
The dying
The freezing
Let me out of here

Stuck in a instrumentality wasteland
The box that can't be repaired
The box made from despair
Created for me from experience
Created by me for resilience

My creation has worked
But where is the end
I will always be boxed
I guess what I made
I made too well

The Box

My life
Closed off
Picked off

Hope you brought me
Life you made me feel
Trapped in a box you see
Takes time for me to heal

This box
With these locks
Slowly being disengaged
Every time I read a page

My life
Crossed off
Ticked off

I'm standing there
Holding my place
Knowing that you care
Not seeing your face

This box
This heavy box
Don't know how it opens
Just more complications

It will be vulnerable
It will be breakable
It will need help
It will need
You

A Puzzle

Like a puzzle
Took me a long time to almost be complete
It was so close to being finished
Becoming such a great picture

Like a puzzle
Over time pieces fell and went missing
The picture would never be full
The image was going to be beautiful

Like a puzzle
Once was supposed to be a life
Now will always be lost forever
All the potential wasted away

Like a puzzle
What could a picture hung on the wall
It is now forgotten, left alone, missing
No one can see the image that once was

Like a puzzle
Left in a box, left on a shelf
Collecting dust, collecting memories
Knowing it will never be complete

Space

Double tap
Screen goes black
White dots fill the view
All is silent
There's no air to breathe

Where is everyone
Nothing that I can feel
To blink and be alone
This has become to real

The dots are so far away
No matter how long I walk
I can't ever reach the stars
They seem to fly past me

Any direction I search
All seems so out of reach
Where do I go to breach
Where do I go to reach

A flickering light becomes close enough
Almost in my grasp
Never close enough

So much pressure coming down on me
Hard to breathe
Gasping for air

Floating along
Feeling alone
Holding on
No where I belong

In the darkness
I'm weightless
In the darkness
I'm anonymous

Left Alone

When is the correct time to scream
When your voice was taken away
Where to show that you can dream
How can you heal with a betray

How do I choose when holding a life
When all I feel is abused and hurt
Holding onto a reminder for life
All I can see is living with a reminder
Might be harder to live with

Where do I go from here
How can I live in fear
How can another care
Can one move past the scare
Would a victim hold onto a life
There's a heart beat that lingers

Do I show a lifetime of hope
When I can barely hold on
Do I give in and give up
When I know there's more to see

Anybody
Can I hold on to
Living in a lie
Living in a cry
Somebody
Can I hold on to
Living in a lie
Living in a cry

Be mindful
But the mind is full of horrors
Be careful
But my cares are wounded

How do I bring new life in
When mine was taking away

My Reflections

No matter how many reflections I see
Yet they all have the same image of me
How do I know which one I will be
Each one shows a different personality

This shows angry
This shows crying
This one is empty
This one is yelling
Yet none show happiness
They all have such darkness

With so many mirrors which one is true
Which one should be shown to you
There's too many emotions here to view
Can I just find one that seems to be new

This shows depressed
This shows anxious
This one is suppressed
This one is clueless
Yet none are cheerful
They all seem so fearful

I know every time I look into this cold lake
There is never a reflection that I recognize
Hope one day that there will be a break
Then the waters will calm down and stabilize

I just want to know which one is me
Which one I should be
To choose accurately
Let me be free

Already Written

I have lived my life to be my best
Seemed understandable
I have felt what happiness is
Seemed unbreakable
Never thought I would lose myself
Seemed unfathomable

Why wasn't there time for my meeting
It was all laid out for me
Just wasn't my time to start breaking
All the failures was meant to be
No sign of all these scars healing
What am I supposed to see

After all the loss
After all the pills
After all the dreams
It's me living in my nightmares

How to fix what's broken
How to breathe after collision
How to grip the chain
It's me living in my skeleton

I want you to know that depression
Isn't an addiction
Just no room for any celebration
So much caution
After all this just one more question
Was this your mission

A Haunted Room

Another day has gone missing
The night slowly came following
It's still me that hasn't been changing
The hauntings are left in the room

I disappear when it goes quiet
Your distraction has been cited
So carefully I walk a tightrope
The hauntings are left in the room

The past shadows burned into the wall
Such a heavy weight pushes down the hall
This air shouldn't be this cold after our fall
The hauntings are left in the room

These vibrations are leaving scars
The echoes press against my fears
Our stillness hovers from the stars
The hauntings are left in the room

It's me who hears the screams
It's me who has those dreams
It's me who lost our themes
The hauntings are left in the room

This War Of Mine

I see you walking in every day
Just slowly showing yourself
I feel my heart beating too fast
It's so hard to move past

Losing a sliver of hope
Everyday I feel your gaze
Breaking off what's left
Everyday I hear your breath

I'm trying to fight
An illness with stress
Im trying to block
Stress with loss

The next step to climb up
Should be easier
I feel the ground trembling
The higher I go
Theres a drag that's pulling me down

The step
The climb
My life
The crumbling
The grinding
My soul

How can I stop something
That fights in the shadows
A darkness that hollows
It's not fair this war wins so often

Where's the light
Where's the support
How to cope with this fight
It's not fair this war wins so often

I feel the darkness taking me
I feel it holding me down
Feeling it surround me
I'm left bare for a war I never asked for

My Night Light

I remember the glass on the floor
The lamp that brought light
Now shattered with red
While I call out I hear nothing

The noise of a hit on the head
The anger I've seen in his eyes
The tears that run down my face
All I want to see is a breath

What brought light to a dark world
The room never felt so cold
Now is in so many pieces
Floor now stained in red

After a breath
We clean up
Soak the glass
Not visible stained
But I know
I can see
Now to rebuild

The reminder has been changed
The light shines again
And the floor been replaced
I can still see all the cracks

After a bad day the light helped
One bad day the light was gone
Again shattered all over
I can see all new scars

While he just sits drinking more
I can see the tears flowing from her
Right there we agreed to leave
Never to look back at our monster

Greed

I've seen greed
I've seen charity
You can chase money
Yet will you never have enough

It's been freed
It's been clarity
It takes your being
Yet you will always want more

Towns have crumbled
Empires have been built
People living in the streets
People live in mansions

Families have starved
Yet we throw our excess
Is there just not enough
Or is there too much

I've seen shelters
I've seen homeless
You will lose yourself
Yet people will always gamble

Driving Hope

Hope always scares me
It ends so poorly
Never-ending cycle
I breathe for a new outlook

Never again will I blink
When you come at me
Never again will I count
When you leave me be

When do you feel fixed up
When I just feel boxed up

I see you on faces of people
I hear your voice when you call
I feel your touch in the wind
If only I can hold onto you

Hope last only a few seconds
It's always gone before it arrives
Just stuck on these islands
Wondering how one survives

Hope
Pushes me forward
Hope
Vision is blurred
Hope
Nothing is pictured
Hope
Just so fractured

When do you feel fixed up
When I just feel boxed up

Hope has made me afraid
Never know what to do
One day I will feel whole
It just won't be today

Damaged Toy

There once was broken toy
Used to bring so much joy
Pretending to be realistic
Even though it was plastic

No matter the damage it suffered
It never once flickered
You couldn't see all the scars
Didn't need to ever replace any parts

Time wasn't kind
He didn't mind
Not always blind
After years of abuse he needed to be
Redesigned

Still all working functions
Just no more expressions
That rarely worked anyways
Not after so many plays

Now it sits all alone
Like it turned to stone
Waiting for what's next in horror
Just my reflection in a mirror

Time wasn't kind
I didn't mind
Not always blind
Years after the abuse I need to be
Redesigned

Ocean Nights

The moon illuminates the ocean
As far I can see
The waves crash with such emotion
Each hit shapes the cliff

Only in silence you can feel it's heart beat
The ocean never sleeps
It's current never seems to be complete
Always shaping the land

To the mysteries the oceans holds
To the lost civilizations
To the ones we lost
How to tame a living, breathing organism

It's the ocean
Always in motion
Never seeks a conclusion
Time breathes the corrosion

The glistening lights it reflexes
Looks as if the deep blue sea weeps

About the Author

Andrew found himself growing up feeling different, never seeming to fit in while being himself. He found comfort in writing and stories he imagined. Writing helped hide away everything that the world gave him.

Andrew Howe

www.ingramcontent.com/pod-product-compliance
Lightning Source LLC
Chambersburg PA
CBHW051324120626
46547CB00015B/2391